youthwriterscamp.com

Greetings to All!

Welcome to those who have decided to give this young author's first book a read. We believe in youth and their stories so much that we believe we can be a part of helping them tell their stories. We have been so inspired to see them grow and change.

Our Youth Writers Camp provides continuous opportunities for healthy emotional expression within a safe and supportive community. Our goal is to both to help young people cope through writing and to motivate them to develop their own streams of revenue.

Brandon C Allen, LLC is actively engaging today's youth with an aim to increase mental and emotional health outcomes. However, we understand that our efforts to positively impact the mental and emotional health of this current generation won't reach maximum effectiveness unless we have the support of the entire community.

THIS IS WHERE YOU COME IN.

Through the things they discovered about themselves, the lessons about mental health, and the coping techniques they garnered during this time, it is our job as a community to continue to cultivate their development and empower them to shift their own realities into the best versions designed for them. Our hope is that these students feel loved, cared for, and equipped enough to continue to heal and process with healthy coping tools and creative avenues. Thank you for investing in this student, one poem at a time.

Students, congratulations and I am proud of all you accomplished. Continue to be all you are meant to be.

Brandon Allen, Author and Founder of Youth Writers Camp

Dear Allyza-Grace,

Do you know what you just did? Seriously. Think about it. You wrote your first book. Did you know that a recent survey of 2,000 U.S. respondents reveals just 15 percent have started writing a book, and a mere six percent have gotten halfway through?

You beat the odds. Many say what they are going to do. Some start it, then abandon it—very few finish. You finished.

Growing up, I always kept a journal. Writing and playing the piano were my first loves. Had I known of a program like this and had a teacher like Brandon Allen, I would have been an author at seven years old. Serving alongside Brandon and making many young authors' dreams come true is a blessing.

Remember, this is just your first step in a long and adventurous journey. Always write. Writing can serve as a constant and reliable best friend.

With love and poetry,

Camari Carter Hawkins
Author and Founder of Mama's Kitchen Press

UNDER PRESSURE
finding my feelings

ALLYZA-GRACE RAMOS

MAMA'S KITCHEN PRESS

Under Pressure: Finding My Feelings
©2023 Allyza-Grace Ramos
ISBN: 979-8-9853373-9-6

First Edition, 2023

Printed in the United States of America

Cover Concept by Allyza-Grace Ramos
Cover & Layout Design by Emily Anne Evans

I would like to dedicate this book to anyone in the world who feels trapped in their own rabbit hole. To anyone who doesn't see how important they are in God's eyes.

I've been there and its okay to not know what you're feeling. Why you're feeling. That's exactly what this book is for: Finding your feelings, and expressing them in a healthy way.

CONTENTS

FOREWORD

Allyza is the youngest of my four daughters. We struggled in our relationship because I am not much of a "feelings" person, and I could not relate to her deep feelings, and we could not be on the same page on this matter. Then, Allyza discovered how to process her emotions through poetry, and this helped her tremendously with her feelings and our relationship improved greatly. It seemed we had a common understanding that, although I provided a lot of ways to help her with her feelings such as physical activities, therapy, and making sure she's connected to a community, I was still not the person to run to with her feelings. Allyza's life experiences at such a young age have forced her to live a life she never wanted. But, instead of staying stuck in the deep hole of depression, she chose to make lemonade out of the lemons that life had thrown at her!

To say "I am proud of you" to my dearest Allyza-Grace would be an understatement! Seeing how much all her hard work of getting out of her dark places has paid off! She never allowed life to beat her. Instead she beat all the trials and, as many as they were, she took every single one by the horns and fought like a warrior! Her middle name "Kemakamepomaika'ilani" means "Precious Blessing From Heaven." She is that and so much more and is showing the world that and so much more!

Lord, I pray for your blessings on *Under Pressure: Finding My Feelings*. Use it to touch the lives of many and bring healing to all who read this book. Lord, use her words to touch hearts and change lives. I pray for freedom for those who are struggling with depression — help bring them out of despair and give them the courage to change that despair to hope. In Jesus name, Amen.

Aileen Whiting

PREFACE

As these past couple of years went by, I've made relationships, lost some, made mistakes, learned lessons, and have been through quite a lot. I wrote this book as a hope to inspire others to pull themselves out of their own rabbit hole. I've been stuck in many and have learned that once your out your gonna want to fall back in. But you can't go back! No matter how big the temptation is. I have really grown in so many different ways these past couple months and I hope my book can be an inspiration to you! Maybe even enough to turn your life around.

No matter how broken you think you are.

UNDER PRESSURE

finding my feelings

THE BREAK UP
(divorce)

where's daddy?
i remember those nights
where i would lay in the middle of the bed
mommy to my left
daddy to my right
in my head
i was the luckiest princess in the world
but little did i know
eventually daddy would have to go
somewhere not too far, but it always felt that way
it was always confusing seeing him once
but not the next day
and it's always the children
that have no clue
about what's yet to come
the things they would have to do
the feelings they would feel
and the trauma they'd have to work through
we're gonna jump to the future for a second
the day i thought would never ever come
finding out that my father had affairs
and it wasn't him my mom found out from
it was what she caught while pregnant
when he decided to be dumb
and it was so hard for little me to believe
that my daddy i thought was so perfect

was just not
i felt my stomach twist
and turn into knots
i couldn't process this
not with all these other thoughts
that daddy had an affair
with not one, but many
i mean, it would've been better
if he didn't have any
as i grew older
i started to wonder and ponder
this vicious thought
that daddy did those things to mommy
because i wasn't good enough
and that hurt
was it my fault that he wasn't satisfied?
that even after all the things they sacrificed
he was still tempted to betray his beautiful bride
are we not enough for you?!
and would we ever be?
maybe
maybe if he had lived to see the look on my face
or maybe if he could physically feel my heart race
we would finally be enough
i guess we'll never know
but if your situation
is anything like mine
know that it is never ever ever the child's fault
no matter what crazy theories you have in mind
like if i hadn't been born
or i should've just listened more.

because everything happens for a reason
it's already set in stone
and it really really sucks
that were the ones that carry it on
those feelings we felt when we were so young
are never really gone
and it causes a lot of things
that we may not even understand
but ur not the only one
i'm here to hold your hand
here to tell you
that there's nothing you could have done
and you don't inherit the sins
from the ones you come from
you are who God made you to be
and no one else
and i hope you one day you are able to accept that
and love yourself.

—

Ephesians 2:10
I am God's poem. Created in Christ Jesus to do
the good things He planned for me long ago.

I JUST WANT TO DIE
(depression and suicidal ideation)

i don't have the energy to get out of the bed today
i'm all out of fake smiles
the ones to show others that i'm okay
you're depressed?
what does that even mean?
it means that your life no longer has value to you
it's not easy being a teen
but they don't know that
they just pretend they do
thinking they know everything you're going through
give your trust to anybody
because they all go on
about how it's going to be okay
"I went through it too, and it never goes away"
maybe you did
but you'll never remember
how i remember that day
maybe it's the same situation
but our pain will never be the same
our demons are different
and mine you cannot tame
so don't even try
my mental health is a player
and my mind is the game
it's tearing my body apart
beating everyone else

and when it gets worse
it brings out a monster
i didn't even know i had in myself
you don't get it.
and it doesn't matter
how many times i have to say it
so don't even try to say you do
it's a different pain
when you no longer want to cry
you just take a deep breath in and accept it
you feel like you're gonna die
and you know it's bad
when you want it to get worse
what's going on with me?
this is no generational curse
yes i know we all struggle
but why do i feel my feelings so strong?
i don't know whats going on
but there's obviously something seriously wrong
i'm struggling every day
and i'm losing hope
i'm drowning in a pool of problems
and i have no way to cope
i can't deal with these lies
constantly filling my mind
i have 20/20 vision
but i can never seem to find
any options other than to not be alive
any other reasons to fight to survive
and i'm failing life miserably
missing all of the times i used to thrive

they're lost in my head somewhere
and they're never coming back
i get so blinded sometimes
everything goes pitch black
this depression is changing me inside and out
i can't seem to find
what all this hype of living is about
i'm okay one second, but i'm not okay the next
my life is escaping me
does this depression define me?
because no matter how hard i try
i can never be the person i always strive to be
i don't know why, but they only choose to see
not my struggles and pain
but times where they saw i was going insane
my cries and my old lies, i'm all out of tries
people come and go
i'm tired of all these goodbyes
my room has no door
but i feel i'm stuck in a jail cell
and if i ever dare to leave
the devil makes my life a living hell
i have many secrets i hide
if you promise not to tell
but don't tell me anything
i don't keep secrets very well
i'd lay in bed at night crying
and i'd toss and i'd turn
staring at the ceiling
waiting to overcome the heartburn
i'd stay up at night

begging for God to take it away
my doctor gave me pills
and my church told me to pray
but nothing made me feel better
so forgive me if i tell you
i don't feel like being alive another day
forgive me if i'm making you sad
when i say nothing is working
i'm better off dead anyway
that is depression
but God wants to fight for you
when you won't even fight for yourself
you are one in a million
you're not "just like everyone else"
and God just wants you to see that
so open up your thoughts, heart and mind
the answer to that heavy feeling in your soul
God will help you find
and He will remove that burden
because that's not your shame to hold
and anyone can surrender
no matter how young or how old

—

Isaiah 41:10
Fear not. For I am with you. Be not dismayed for I am
your God. I will strengthen you. Yes, I will help you. Yes I
will uphold you with the right hand of my righteousness.

NO CONTROL
(anxiety and overthinking)

i have no control
my anxiety is holding the reins
making all the decisions
dealing with all the pains
but i would like to try to be in control
maybe just one time
but whenever i try
they make it feel like i'm committing a crime
they also don't like
when people raise their voice
no one else can do it
unless it's their choice
they really like to argue and yell
so they're definitely a little hypocritical
if you couldn't already tell
but i want to be in control
making decisions for myself
i can't let my life be taken by anyone else
so i try to remind myself
of 1 Peter 5:7
cast all your anxiety on Him
because He cares for you
if i can take my life back
so can you
so send your anxiety
right back to where it came from

send them back to the gates of hell
and tell satan that you are done
done letting him tell you you're not good enough
or that nobody likes you
that you're better off dead
and there's nothing you can do
because you know your worth
and if you don't, then i'll tell you
you are worth so much
that God is on your side
He wants your heart, soul, and your mind
that empty feeling inside of you
He will help you find
and He will fill you with his grace
because He wants all of you
the good and the bad
the times you're happy and the times you're sad
all of the memories you shoved deep down inside
and all the burdens from the past
that you've tried to hide
He wants it
because you are more important
than all the luggage you carry
so give God a chance
even if it seems scary
every day looking on
every obstacle you come upon
God will be there
He loves every flaw or insecurity
because that's what makes you different
from everyone else

including me
and here's a piece of advice
from the girl who got smarter not harder:
it's gonna get ugly
before it gets better
sometimes you can't do it alone, but you have me
and we'll do it together

—

1 Peter 5:7
Give all your anxiety to God for He cares about you.

BEHIND THE SCREEN
(social media)

you're on your technology
every chance of the day you can get
sometimes a little too much
it's easy to forget
all of the things that you have to do
and so much time passes by
i know because i do it too
and i don't know why
but how do you even tell
between what's fake and what's real?
people lie about their feelings all the time
even if it's the opposite of how they really feel
it's so easy to deceive someone
you can be anything or anyone
you want people to believe
but you have to be real smart
to actually see
to see what's really going on behind the screen
photoshop. editing. the endless possibilities.
gen z is not your normal type of teen
so don't be tricked or
start to wish that you were someone else
be careful what you wish for
trust me, it's easier to be yourself
and though it might not seem that way
everything's going to be okay

as long as you stop telling yourself
to start doing something about it tomorrow
instead of starting today
so get off your phone
don't be the person hiding behind the screen
and don't worry about what you look like
just be who you truly want to be
without leading people on
or showing them the parts
that only you want them to see
if everyone just started embracing
who they truly are
this world could be so much better
society can go so far
so instead of hiding behind a filter
or spending all your time editing a picture
life is gonna pass you by
and you're gonna wish things could go back
to the way they were
so do something about it
social media is a hole
once you're in you can't get out
people changing their lives to match what's "IN"
what's that all about?
and people believe it
but they just don't see
a kind act
may be more than what it appears to be
it's hard to believe
whats fake and what's true
that everyone has an insecurity

including me too
society has these expectations
that everyone thinks they have to follow
but society doesn't understand
the facts of how hard it is to swallow
when you don't look like
the fake edited girls on a magazine
when you've struggled with things
you should never have to go through
your mental understanding the age of an adult
when you're still just a teen
some social media is real
but everyone makes mistakes
are you just gonna let others suffer
at the hands of social media
or are you gonna do whatever it takes
to spread love and positivity
whenever you can
because it will multiply
and do things you never thought possible
that's my plan

—

Ephesians 4:25
Having put away falsehood, let each one of you speak the truth
with his neighbor, for we are members one of another.

SCARS
(self-harm)

why can't i scar?
did i not cut deep enough
or is the blade not sharp enough
to cut through the skin
i thought was too tough?
maybe i'm just not strong enough
not strong enough
to handle the pain
but also not strong enough
to cut deeper through my veins
i have friends that cut too deep
they've gone too far
as i'm trying to pull them back
but the devil is pulling harder
he's a real maniac
and i was terrified
because going there
means you don't know if you're coming back
the pain that i felt was so unbearable
and there's no planning for that
God i would do anything
to rewind back the time
so maybe i could find any hint or clue
that could help in the future
so that when i look back
i could say that i helped her get better

but it doesn't work that way.
i wish the temptation could just go away
i wish i didn't have to worry
about the objects around me all day
led pencils, sharpeners, rubber bands
my mind is pretty creative
so nothing's allowed in my hands
and if it comes down to it
and i end up giving in
i feel guilty
and beg the Lord my God
to forgive me of my sin
only the next day
to do the same thing anyway
and it hurts me more
than it hurts everyone else
but just not enough
to be able to stop myself
i have to sit in the unsatisfied
the parts where i long for more
when the memories of the cut won't suffice
i relapse
because there's no other act as satisfying
than what self-harm has in store
as slitting my wrists
or giving myself a bruise
cutting off my circulation
self-harm has become my muse
and once ur addicted
there's no turning around
i'm trying to climb out of this rabbit hole

but i keep getting pushed down
and it doesn't help
that though i'm not the only one feeling this way
my mom's constantly giving me lectures
and making me feel like i'm going insane
i feel like i've let her down
i'm not the child she pictured i was gonna be
i'm sorry mom
that you didn't get some perfect little kid
you got me
but i'm trying my best
to fill your expectations
and impress you
but it's hard to want to try that hard
when i'm struggling too
it's getting too hard
i mean
what am i supposed to do with this feeling?
what if maybe i'm not ready
to start the process of healing?
that's okay
when i'm ready i'll know
because sometimes you have to hold on
in order to let go
If you're feeling this way
when you're ready you'll know what to do
and don't think God won't be there
He's walking this journey right next to you

—

James 4:8
Come near to God and He will come near to you

18

EPISODES
(panic attacks)

what does it feel like to have a panic attack?
it feels like you're fighting for your life
not ever knowing if you're coming back
my heart starts to race, my body starts to pace
i wish i was somebody else
but that's not the case
my head is spinning and i can't see straight
i wish i could turn away
but everything's happened so fast, it's too late
too late to turn around
back to where it's safe and sound
i'm afraid i've strayed too far
lost and never to be found
i fall into this never-ending state of panic
i'm silently screaming
making myself feel manic
but i can't shake this feeling out
it's not going away
there's nothing you can do, nothing you can say
to ever make it okay
i'm losing my breath slowly
and i'm barely hanging on
i wish i had the strength i did when i was young
but i'm afraid that's gone.
my body feels numb from the constant shake
i don't know how much longer i have

until i give up
i don't know how much more my body can take
i start to feel lightheaded
like i'm about to collapse
sometimes this goes on for hours
i never know how long it's gonna last
and all you can do to help me
is just wait for it to pass
i'm sitting there crying, i feel like i'm dying
i'm sorry i'm like this
but i swear i'm trying
as fear starts to close in
i can't help but feel that i will never win
i never know how to stop
but i also don't know how to begin
i can never seem to find the light
everyone claims i hold within
my body goes tight, nothing feels right
i'm so exhausted
i have no energy to fight
my heart hurts too much
and i just want it stop
it feels like my head is too full
and it's about to pop
i've never felt so alone though i'm surrounded
and i'm doing fine on my own
but i can't help, but not feel grounded
my emotions get the best of me
and i feel like a caged-up bird
left with no key
no one around to see

never ever to be set free
a sharp pain in my chest
is it ever gonna end?
my heart is too cracked
to even try to mend
i try to stand up, but all i do is fall down
my visions are too blurred
i can't see what's around
all i hear is voices
telling me to breathe in and out
one. two. three.
telling me to open my eyes
so i can see
but i just shut them tighter
the voices start to get quieter
the pain in my heart lighter
i guess i am a fighter.
it may not feel like it
but in the end it'll be okay
ready to start fresh the next day
because panic is temporary
and doesn't last forever
and one day it'll become just a memory
one you won't remember

—

Isaiah 35:4
Say to those who have an anxious heart, "Be strong; fear not! Behold, your God will come with vengeance, with the recompense of God. He will come and save you."

MEMORIES THAT EAT ME
(ptsd)

heart beats faster
i can't see straight
it's always the ones i don't see coming
the memories i underestimate
the ones i didn't think mattered
because they didn't make me feel some way
but somehow
those ones bring me back to that day
making me relive the past
but i guess it's easier now
knowing it's not going to last
but it's terrifying to look back
and remember how it made me feel
and it's not some illusion in my mind
and sometimes i can't keep a promise
though i would like to
i'm a ticking time bomb
and letting it out is the only thing i can do
because i can't hold it in and if i even try
anything would be better than that pain
even if it meant i had to die
in the moment i tell myself it's just a memory
that everything's going to be okay
eventually
i start to sweat and i start to feel hot
my body thinks that this is very real

but it's actually not
it just gets hard to tell
with all the suffering and the pain
and even though i know it's over
i feel like i'm going insane
people always ask me how i'm doing
and i just say i'm okay
because even though i'm in pain
i know there's nothing they could do
to take it away
i wish i could tell you it only happens one time
but to lead you to such pain
would be a crime
it's gonna happen when you least expect it
so always be prepared
and when it does come
don't be scared
because you're not alone
even though it feels that way
there are people that love you
and everything's going to be okay

—

Romans 1:18
*God knows about the trauma experienced by every
single person. He knows the details of how the
trauma came about, and He hates the wickedness
that caused such pain. Take heart in knowing that God
comforts us. He is close to the brokenhearted and
comforts us when we suffer, holding us in His arms.*

DADDY ISSUES
(attention)

what do they mean to me?
for me...
it means you struggle with craving attention
especially when it's from guys
and it's hard for people to trust you
when they look at past lies
you were constantly tripping up
and you're all out of tries
you probably have a lot of guy friends
but have a crush on one, two, or even three
and you get so blinded
by getting that satisfaction
it's hard to see
when someone is being true
or just taking advantage of you
it's okay because i've been through it too
i'm only thirteen, but my mind is older
and the further i let myself go
my heart just grew colder
i'm writing this poem
mostly about what i've personally been through
when there were times where i had to choose
between a good and bad choice
and i didn't know what to do
i've struggled where i've put my attention
giving my heart out to guys and getting attached

but i guess you can't listen to your heart
because i was always mismatched
struggling with feeling complete
an empty hole in my heart
i looked for it in the wrong places
my life slowly started falling apart
at first i didn't know why
then i figured out that part of it was my dad
that i never saw or appreciated
the love i already had
the poem about divorce earlier in the book
talks about him
going back to the start of days
that were always grim
he had affairs with other women
letting them into the bed
and as a little girl
it really messed with my head
and i guess as i got older
it made me think
that being with guy to guy was okay
well, i knew it wasn't okay
but i wanted to feel full for even just a second
and i did it anyway
i was attracted to older men
who took advantage of me
i also tried relationships with guys the same age
only to find out a lot of them were just a fantasy
i could be anyone i wanted to be
thought right now i'm taking a break
and if i do, i date to marry

but right now
i'm putting down all the relationships
i thought i had to carry
for the first time in my life
i finally feel free
i can show everyone the person
i want and am trying to be
and it feels good
so if you're struggling too
let God into your heart
and let Him be a good father to you
doing things that make you happy
getting satisfaction from that
and if i can tell you one thing to remember...
is to never go back
because i know it feels safe
and the temptation's still there
it's easier to just go back
but to me, that's not fair
even though it's hard
it's not worth giving in
because the devil can't win
unless you give into sin

—

2 Corinthians 6:18
And I will be your Father, and you will be my
sons and daughters, says the Lord Almighty.

ONCE UPON A LOVE STORY
(love and heartbreak)

have you ever felt so in love with somebody
you thought you'd be with them
for the rest of your life?
until they say the words
you'd never thought they'd say
the ones that cut deeper than a knife
like one being
"i have feelings for someone else"
and the worst part is
you loved them more
than you could ever love yourself
and you thought they did too
or they say
"sorry, this isn't gonna work out"
though the other day, they said "i love you" first
what was that all about?
oh, here's another one
"i don't see us having a future together,
you were living in a fantasy"
whatever. but not too long ago
you said you wanted that fantasy with me
yeah, all those words and more
relationships ended in seconds
what was all that effort for?
they didn't feel that way before
you claim it's fine

you know there will be another coming your way
and though the pain is unimaginable
you say you'll be okay
because it's happened before
with another person in the past
and sometimes you're with people
even though you know it's not gonna last
because when love comes
heartbreak follows soon after
those memories bring sadness
instead of bringing laughter
the pain brings feelings
you never ever thought you'd feel
and you can't accept the fact
that maybe your love wasn't real
in the moment it felt like it could be
and the memories you had felt like enough proof
that the love you shared was so strong
strong enough to be bulletproof
i guess it wasn't
i didn't know what love felt like until i met you
but now i know what a broken heart feels like too
that hits so hard
when i'm drowning in my feelings
laying in my bed,
staring at the ceiling
wondering if i'm ever gonna be ready
to start my process of healing
onto the next relationship
preparing myself for the next broken heart
and maybe in the future.

i wont have to worry about that part
they'll probably come when i'm not looking for one
so i'm just waiting for that day
for now i don't have to worry
about love and broken hearts
and if i ever do
i know it'll be okay
when my heart is heartbroken
and i don't know what to do with the little bit
i'll give it to my Heavenly Father
because i know He'll take good care of it

—

Psalm 147:3
He heals up the brokenhearted and binds up their wounds.

DIVING DEEP AND RETURNING TO SHORE
(water)

how deep can i go and still return to shore?
if i go too deep
what will i lose, how will i gain more?
my head is spinning, my body is sinking
i'm trying to survive
but my mind goes blank thinking
but still filled with the thought
that maybe this is where i belong
that i've been banished to pain
for the rest of my life
because i just wasn't that strong
i start to calm my breath down
and i open my eyes to see
this perfect world i've entered into
is way better than reality
these emotions get the best of me
sometimes i don't feel i am the best i can be
am i enough to return back from the deep?
giving God the pain that i chose to keep
it's not his burden, though they say it is not mine
is it really a burden at all?
or just another lesson in life
very unfortunate people find?
how do i comfortably sit with the fact

that i could've done more
all the times before i relapsed and went back
is when i was supposed to use the energy
i saved in store
i hate giving it to him
knowing i didnt try my best
but i think surrendering it to him
when you can't carry it all
is the real test
i start to feel the sand under my toes again
as i reminisce on the memories of the deep
my mind starts to wonder
how much further does it go?
and if i go too far
can i still return to shore?
yes, i can
though i was struggling, i was still alive
my heart still beating
inside i knew i would survive
holding out on hope made my body grow strong
and it's made me feel safe knowing
sometimes it's okay to be wrong
but how did i stray so far
from the places
where i could stand with my head above water?
where gravity does all the work
and i don't have to work any harder
i'm terrified of falling back down the rabbit hole
all the memories flashing back
on all the things the devil stole
making me feel like i wasn't good enough

for things i wanted to do
and there was still pain and trauma
i could never get through
i never want to backtrack
letting the devil take control of me
i'm coming back the total opposite
of who he wanted me to be
but if and when i do go back
to where my toes don't reach the sand
God will love me through it all and hold my hand
for He is the reason i return to shore
so if and when i do go back
i will know how to battle what may be next in store

—

Isaiah 43:2
When you go through deep waters, I will be with you.
When you go through rivers of difficulty, you will not
drown. When you walk through the fire of oppression, you
will not be burned up; the flames will not consume you.

ACKNOWLEDGMENTS

I have a lot of people I would like to mention in this book, but I want to start with God. None of this would be possible without Him. He's helped me heal the parts of me I thought were gonna be broken forever, and I am forever grateful for Him!

I would also like to acknowledge my mom. She brought me into this world and has supported me and my dreams my whole life. I know I am difficult and she never gave up on me. We have had our ups and downs, but I am so glad I get to be called her daughter.

To my dad, I am also mentioning him. Though he is deceased he will always hold a very special place in my heart. Thank you for being my father. I will always be your princess!

I'm acknowledging my therapist, Donna. There have been many times where I have fallen back but she never stops believing in me. She came in a really hard time in my life, and has been there through the good and the bad. Giving me the spiritual advice I need to push myself, and the motivation to actually do it. Thank you Donna!

I want to acknowledge all of my sisters too. Laci, she's not my blood sister but she does treat me like her little sister. Kerri, my oldest and "favorite sister". I'm just kidding, maybe. She's like my mom, best friend, and sister all in one! Lourdes, she's the sister I'm not really close to but I really do enjoy our conversations. She's so wise and really helps me look at situations from different points of view. Finally, Jana. It's hard to describe her, she's the sister who loves to make fun of me, call me names, and make me cry sometimes. But, she is also the sister I dance, scream songs with, and who pulls me out of my feelings. So thank you to all of my beautiful sisters!

I want to acknowledge my church. To all the family and friends who have supported me as my church, who have been there though my high and lows, never doubting me. That includes my pastor, youth pastor, my leader Angie, youth group girls, my fellow volunteers and my "Girl Gang".

I also want to acknowledge the person wrote the words for the back of this book, my soul sister, Zoe. She's another sister, best friend, and someone who keeps my life in check. My protector and guardian. She also writes poetry and that is why I asked her to give you a glimpse inside my book. Thank you Zoe.

ABOUT THE AUTHOR

Hello! My name is Allyza-Grace Kemakamae pomaika 'i lani Ramos. I was born in Honolulu, Hawaii on October 29th, 2009. I moved to California when I was seven after my dad passed away. Poetry has recently become an outlet for my feelings. When I am feeling a strong emotion about a situation I just write a poem about it, and it just comes naturally.

www.ingramcontent.com/pod-product-compliance
Lightning Source LLC
Chambersburg PA
CBHW060509300726
48975CB00008B/2710